Bible Heroes— Parables of Jesus

Read and Do Activities
by Mary E. Lysne

These stories are fun and easy to read.
A picture stands for a word.

STANDARD
PUBLISHING
Cincinnati, Ohio

ISBN 0-7847-0102-4
The Standard Publishing Company, Cincinnati, Ohio.
A division of Standex International Corporation.
© 1993 by Mary E. Lysne
Printed in the United States of America
23-02582

Tell Me a Story

 Bible   Jesus   God   teach   temple   stories   seeds   boat lesson

When?   In times.

Who?   , 's Son.   was a er.   He

started ing when he was only 12!   taught

ers in the .   He called it , "My Father's work."

How?   .   told  called parables.

were about sheep.   And .   And money.

Where?   Anywhere.   On the sea.   In the .   On

hills.   In s.   At meals.

What?   s.   weren't just for fun.   They

were s about s about 's

kingdom.   s about how to live.

Why?   To teach hard things.   Parables were simple.

The stories made hard lessons easy.

Picture Crossword

The words in this puzzle are from "Tell Me a Story." The clues are pictures. What words go with the clues? Write them in the empty boxes.

Clues Across

2.

4.

6.

7.

10. **12**

11.

Clues Down

1.

3.   5.   8.

4. **abc** er   6.    9.

Bird Seed

Jesus Lake Galilee people boat plant grain seeds bird rocks

One day 🧎 was at 🏞. Many 🧎 came to 🏞. They came to hear 🧎. 🧎 got into a 🛶. He told this story. "A farmer 🌱ed 🌾 ⋰⋱. Some ⋰⋱ fell by the road. 🐦s came. The 🐦s ate the ⋰⋱. Some ⋰⋱ fell on 🪨. Small 🌱s grew and died. Some ⋰⋱ fell among weeds. Small 🌱s grew. Weeds grew. The small 🌱s died. Some ⋰⋱ fell on good ground. Small 🌱s grew. And grew. They turned into 🌾. The 🌾 made more 🌾." What do you think 🧎' lesson means? The ⋰⋱ are God's words. The ground is 🧎. The 🐦s and weeds are bad. They keep 🧎 from believing God's words. "Listen. Understand. Obey God's words," 🧎 said.

Star and Box

Inside this star are words from the story "Bird Seed."
Find the words from the story.   Draw boxes around
them.   Cross out the words that are not in the story.

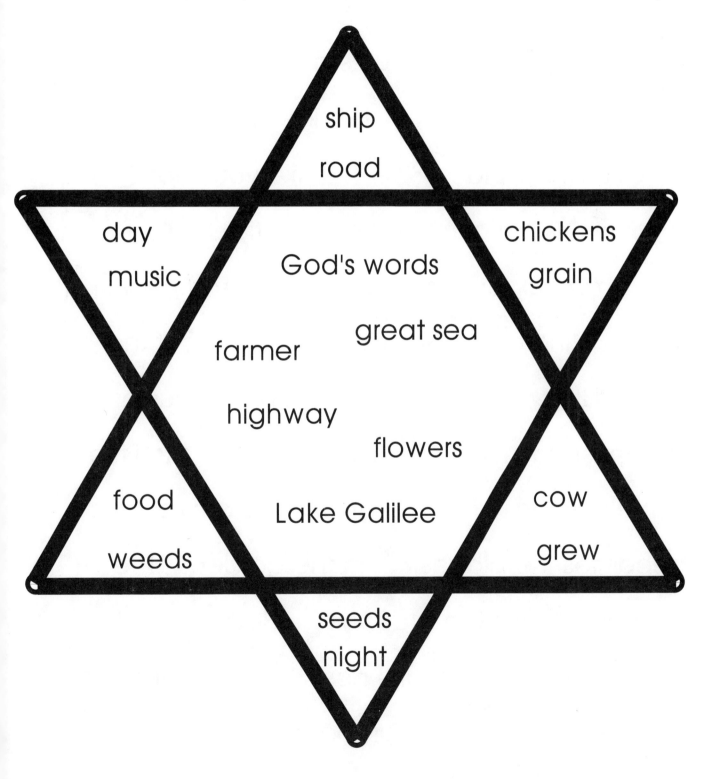

ship
road

day
music

chickens
grain

God's words

great sea

farmer

highway

flowers

food

Lake Galilee

cow

weeds

grew

seeds
night

The Kingdom of Heaven

God   king   kingdom   seed   bread   treasure   fish   plant   bird

[God] is a [king]. A [king] rules a [kingdom]. [God]'s [kingdom] is the [kingdom] of Heaven. "[God]'s [kingdom] is like a mustard [seed]," Jesus said. "And [God]'s [kingdom] is like yeast for [bread]. [God]'s [kingdom] is like a [treasure] hidden in a field. [God]'s [kingdom] is like a man looking for fine pearls. And [God]'s [kingdom] is like a [fish]ing net." Here is the story about the mustard [seed]. The [kingdom] of [God] is like a mustard [seed]. The mustard [seed] is very small. You [plant] the little [seed] in the garden. The [seed] grows and grows. It becomes the biggest [plant] in the garden. The mustard [plant] has big branches. How big? Big enough for [bird]s to make nests in it. What does this mean? Small things can become very big.

Find Two the Same

Two treasure chests on this page are exactly the same. Color the two that are the same. Put an X on the four treasure chests that are different.

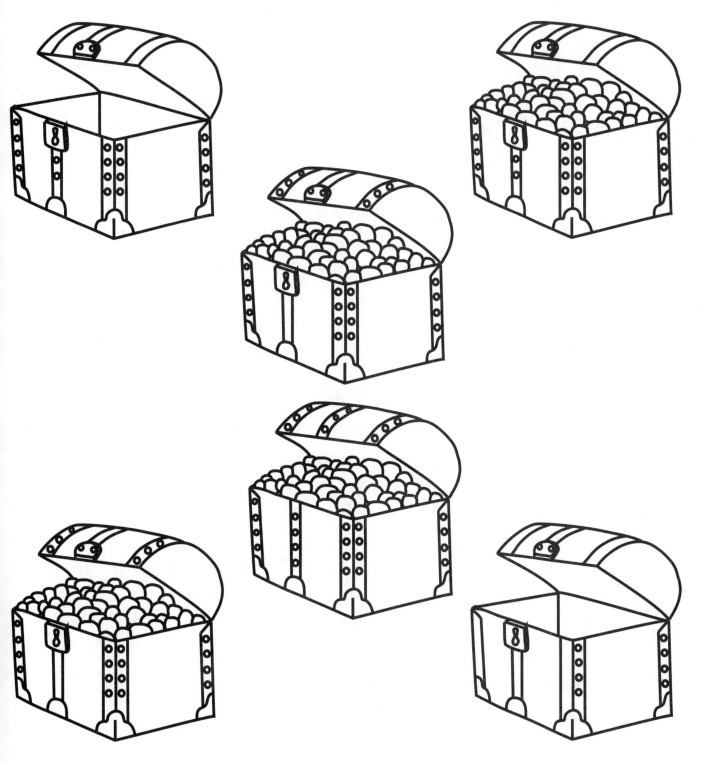

Not Enough

people   Jesus   sin   man   sheep   one   home   look   happy   heart

Some [people] made fun of [Jesus]. "[Jesus] makes friends with [sin]ners," they said. So [Jesus] told them this story. A [man] has 100 [sheep]. 1 [sheep] gets lost. 99 [sheep] are still enough, right? No! The [man] leaves his 99 [sheep] safe at [home]. He [look]s for the 1 lost [sheep]. He [look]s until he finds it. "Then he is very [happy]," [Jesus] said. He puts the [sheep] on his shoulders and goes [home]. At [home] the [man] calls his friends. "Be [happy] with me. I found my lost [sheep]!" the [man] says. What do you think [Jesus]' story means? The 1 lost [sheep] is a [sin]ner. The [sin]ner changes his [heart]. God saves him. What a [happy] place Heaven is! Why? Because 1 lost [sin]ner changed his [heart]. Because God loves everyone.

Color It

White clouds and sheep. Blue sky. Green grass.
Brown fence. Choose your favorite colors to color
this picture of sheep and shepherds.

Please Forgive

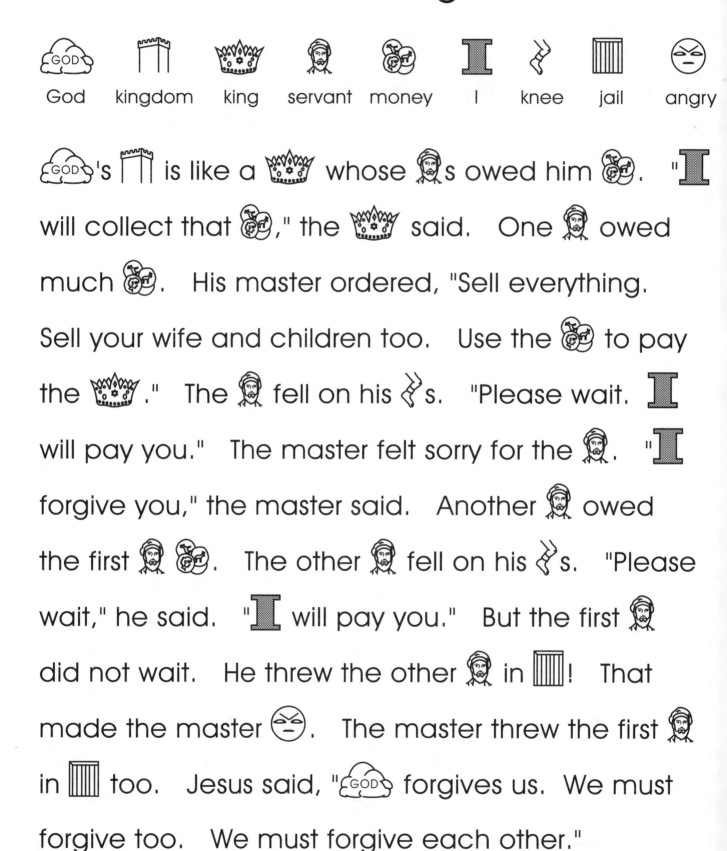

God   kingdom   king   servant   money   I   knee   jail   angry

God's kingdom is like a king whose servants owed him money. "I will collect that money," the king said. One servant owed much money. His master ordered, "Sell everything. Sell your wife and children too. Use the money to pay the king." The servant fell on his knees. "Please wait. I will pay you." The master felt sorry for the servant. "I forgive you," the master said. Another servant owed the first servant money. The other servant fell on his knees. "Please wait," he said. "I will pay you." But the first servant did not wait. He threw the other servant in jail! That made the master angry. The master threw the first servant in jail too. Jesus said, "God forgives us. We must forgive too. We must forgive each other."

Dots and Lines

Every letter has lines, dots, or lines with dots to take its place.   When you spell DOG, it looks like □ ⌊• ⋮⋮ . The dots and lines in the middle box spell out a message about God.   Can you figure it out?

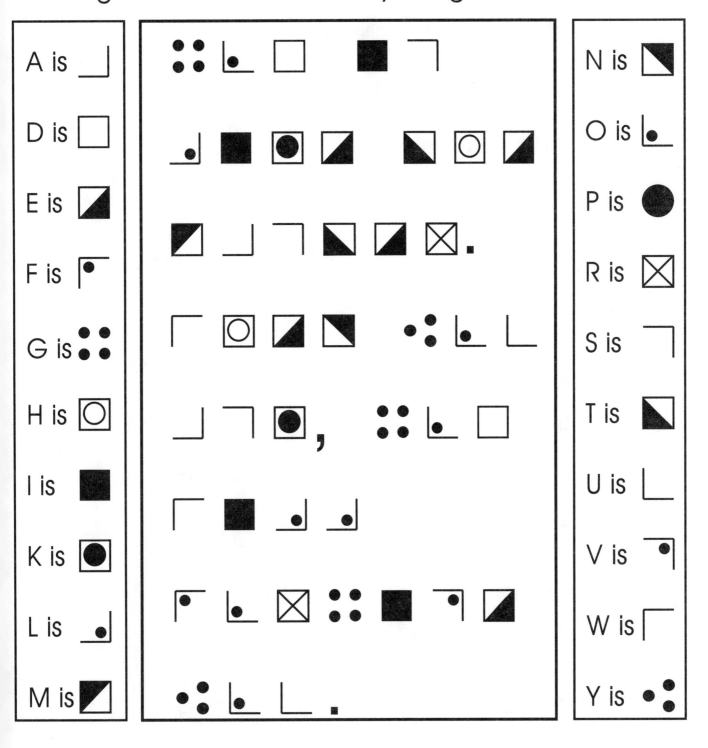

Ten Young Ladies

Jesus   **ten**   **girl**   **lamp**   **oil**   **night**   **shout**   **meal**   **door**

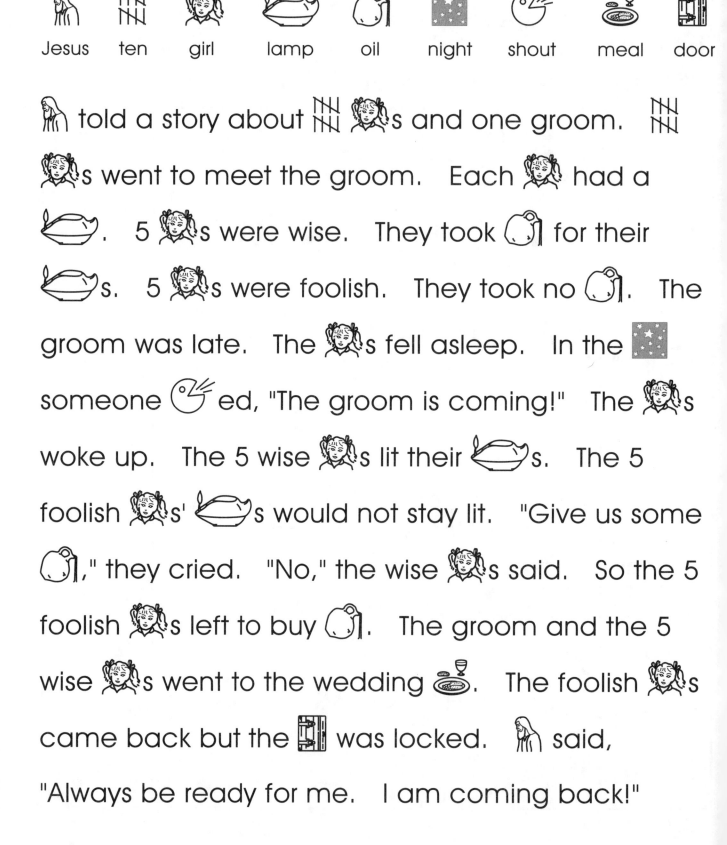

(Jesus) told a story about (ten) (girl)s and one groom. (ten) (girl)s went to meet the groom. Each (girl) had a (lamp). 5 (girl)s were wise. They took (oil) for their (lamp)s. 5 (girl)s were foolish. They took no (oil). The groom was late. The (girl)s fell asleep. In the (night) someone (shout)ed, "The groom is coming!" The (girl)s woke up. The 5 wise (girl)s lit their (lamp)s. The 5 foolish (girl)s' (lamp)s would not stay lit. "Give us some (oil)," they cried. "No," the wise (girl)s said. So the 5 foolish (girl)s left to buy (oil). The groom and the 5 wise (girl)s went to the wedding (meal). The foolish (girl)s came back but the (door) was locked. (Jesus) said, "Always be ready for me. I am coming back!"

Marriage Maze

Ten girls went to a wedding. Only five girls can go in. Help the five girls get into the wedding to meet the groom. Draw a path through the maze.

start

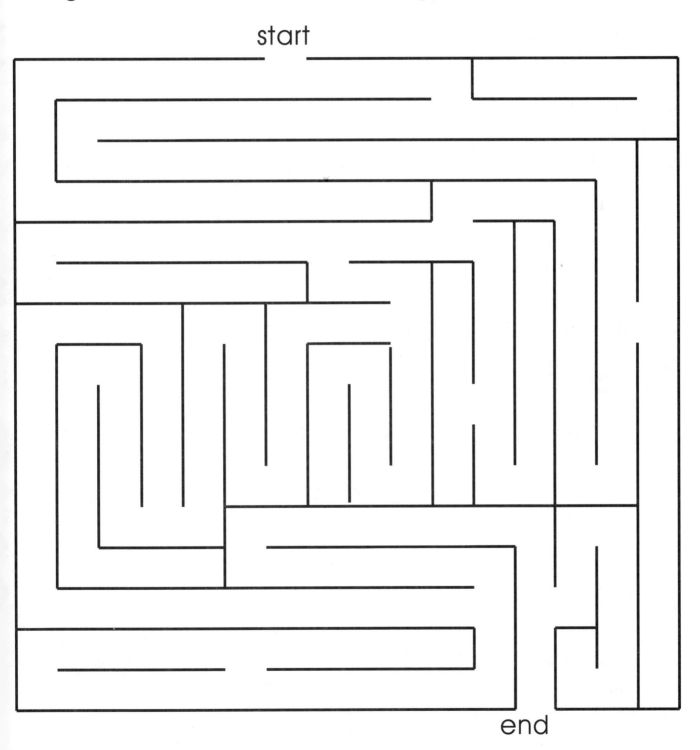

end

Midnight Visitor

U = you $\begin{smallmatrix}+2\\1\\=?\end{smallmatrix}$ = problem   🍞 = bread   🚦 = go   💡 = idea   ▨ = night   🚪 = door   🛏 = bed   ☁GOD = God

"Let's pretend," Jesus said. Pretend **U** are grown up and a friend comes to visit **U**. That's fun, but **U** have a $\frac{+2}{1}=?$. **U** are out of 🍞. What can **U** do? 🚦 without 🍞? No! That's not a good 💡. Borrow some 🍞? Good 💡! Now **U** have another $\frac{+2}{1}=?$. It's ▨. How do you borrow 🍞 at ▨? **U** 🚦 to a friend. Knock, knock on the friend's 🚪. "I have a visitor. I'm out of 🍞. Please give me some 🍞," **U** say. "🚦 away," the friend says. "I am in 🛏." Now what? Give up? No! **U** knock again. The 🚪 swings open. The friend gives you 🍞. What does this story mean? Ask ☁GOD. ☁GOD gives us what we need.

The Answer Is . . .

Here are five questions and answers from the story "Midnight Visitor." The <u>answers</u> are given. Can you guess what the <u>questions</u> are?

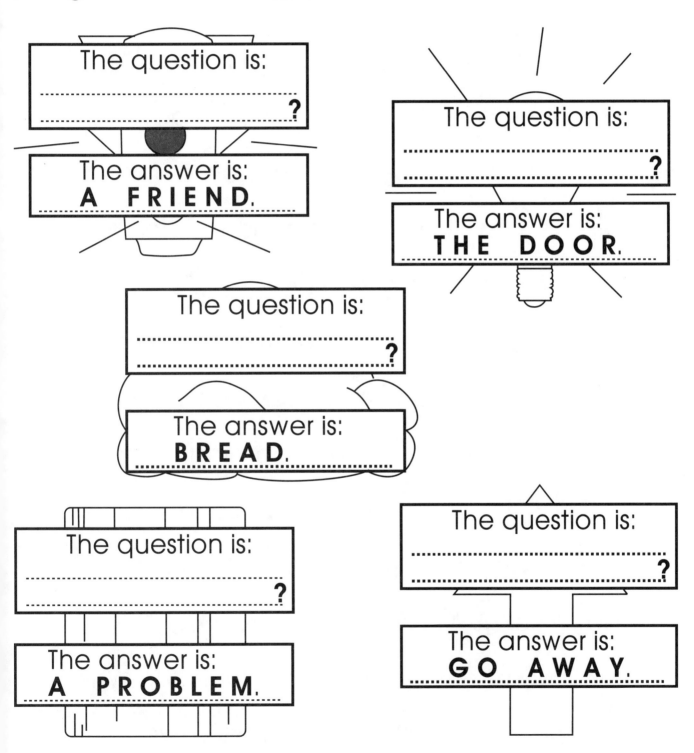

The question is:
....
.... ?

The answer is:
A FRIEND.

The question is:
....
.... ?

The answer is:
THE DOOR.

The question is:
....
.... ?

The answer is:
BREAD.

The question is:
....
.... ?

The answer is:
A PROBLEM.

The question is:
....
.... ?

The answer is:
GO AWAY.

Pig Food

son   father   home   money   food   pig   idea   happy   remember

A 🧑 once said to his 🧕, "I want to leave 🏠. Give me my share of the 💰." The 🧕 gave his 🧑 the 💰. The 🧑 left 🏠. He had lots of fun. He spent all his 💰. Then he got hungry. No 💰! No 🍲! The 🧑 got a job giving 🍲 to 🐖s. Slop, slop. The 🐖 🍲 looked good enough to eat. At last he had an 💡. "My 🧕 has enough 🍲. I'll go 🏠." So he did. 🧕 saw him coming. "I'm sorry, 🧕," the 🧑 said. "I have sinned. Let me serve you." 🧕 hugged his 🧑. "Let's have a feast," 🧕 ordered. "Be 🙂," he said to everyone. "My 🧑 was lost. Now he is found." 🪢 this truth: When you change your heart, God will forgive you.

Dot-to-Dot

Can you count from 1 to 91? Then you can do this dot-to-dot. Draw lines to connect the dots. Color the picture. Use the picture to tell a story.

Riches and Rags

🛍️ rich   ♡ love   💰 money   🧥 clothes   ☁️GOD God   🍲 food   🪦 die   🔥 fire   ✋ help

"Once a poor man lived near a 🛍️ man. The 🛍️ man ♡d 💰. He wore only the best 🧥. The poor man was Lazarus. He owned nothing. But he ♡d ☁️GOD. Lazarus went to the 🛍️ man's home. He asked the 🛍️ man for a little 🍲. Do you think the 🛍️ man give him 🍲? No. When Lazarus 🪦d, ☁️GOD took him to Heaven to be with Abraham. When the 🛍️ man 🪦d, he went to a place of 🔥. The 🛍️ man could see Lazarus. "✋ me," he said. "I'm thirsty. This 🔥 hurts." Abraham answered, "You did not ✋ Lazarus. Now I cannot ✋ you." What could Jesus' story mean? Do not ♡ 💰 more than ☁️GOD. ✋ your neighbor if you can.

Numbers and Letters

Every letter in a box has a number.   Every line has a number too.   Match the numbers.   Then write the matching letters on the lines.   Some letters are not used!

29. ⊘	13. P	54. T	45. R	46. E	23. J	22. O	7. T	33. Y	50. D
9. W	10. O	58. G	2. F	32. C	8. H	59. V	12. ⊠M	3. Q	49. A
30. L	15. K	34. Y	57. O	11. E	27. L	28. I	43. G	42. E	36. I
37. M	44. O	40. S	6. M	18. T	25. S	16. E	14. L	35. H	21. B
19. O	52. L	47. D	55. N	4. R	20. V	41. O	48. U	26. J	31. H
56. C	38. N	60. O	1. W	53. I	5. E	51. O	17. X	24. M	39. Y

Write the matching letters here.

__	__		__	__		__	__	__	__	__	__	__
53.	18.		28.	40.		2.	57.	22.	14.	36.	25.	8.

__	__		__	__	__	__	M	__	__	__	__
54.	19.		27.	41.	20.	5.	12.	44.	55.	46.	33.

__	O	__	__		__	__	__	__		__	__	__
24.	29.	4.	42.		7.	31.	49.	38.		34.	51.	48.

__	__	__	__		__	__	__	▪
30.	60.	59.	16.		43.	10.	50.	

Sacks and Sacks

important   king   ten   servant   sack   money   cities   angry   God

An 🎖️ man got ready for a trip. When he came back, he would be 👑. Before he left, he called to his 🔟 servant s. "Here is a 💰 of 💵 for each of you. Use it. Make more 💵 with it." Then the 🎖️ man went on his trip. He became 👑 and came back. "Come here," the 👑 said to the 🔟 servant s. "How much 💵 did you make?" he asked. One 🧕 said, "I made 🔟 💰 s of 💵." "Good," the 👑 said. "You will rule 🔟 🏙️." One 🧕 said, "I made 5 💰 s of 💵." "Good," the 👑 said. "You will rule 5 🏙️." One 🧕 said, "I didn't even try. I hid the 💵." The 👑 was 😠 and took his 💵 back. Jesus means this: Obey 🌥️GOD. Use what 🌥️GOD gives you.

Silly Sacks

Ten sacks for you.   And ten for you.   And ten for
you.   The king gave out sacks and sacks of money.
How many sacks can you find on this page?

A Good Neighbor

man   Jesus   Jew   up   priest   stop   medicine   inn   love

"Who is my neighbor?" a [man] asked [Jesus]. [Jesus] told him this story. Once a [Jew]ish [man] walked along a road. Some robbers came and beat the [man] [up]. The [man] was almost dead. Soon a [Jew]ish [priest] came. The [priest] did not [stop] to help. Next a [priest]'s helper came. He looked at the [man]. He did not [stop] either. Later a person the [Jew]s hated came. He looked at the [man]. He felt sorry for him. He put some [medicine] on his sores. Then the enemy took him to an [inn]. "I will pay you to care for him," he said to the [inn]keeper. [Jesus] asked, "Now which [man] was his neighbor?" The one who helped him! [Jesus] said, "Go and do the same. [love] your neighbor. Help people in need."

Stop and Search

Up, down, backwards, forwards.   Look in all directions for the word SORRY and 9 other 5-letter words from the story "A Good Neighbor."

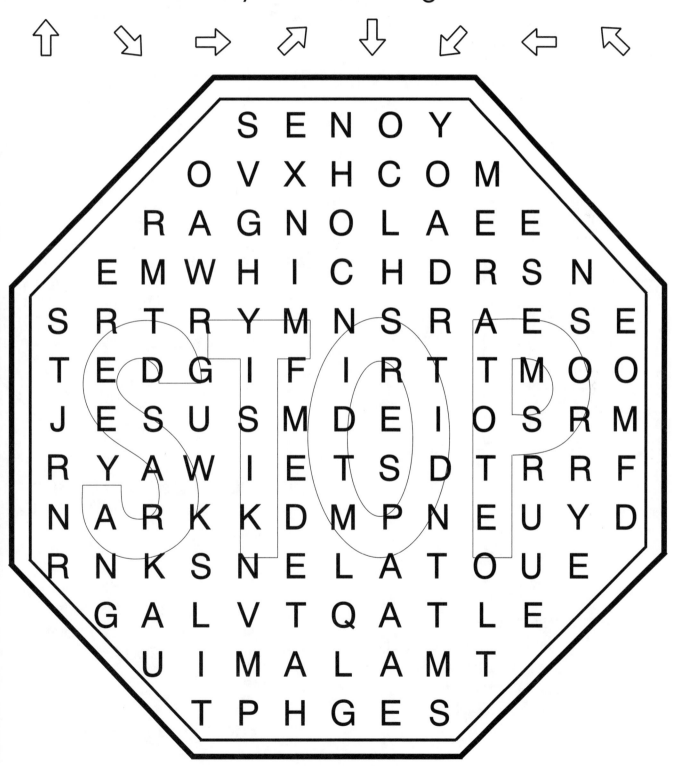

```
        S E N O Y
        O V X H C O M
      R A G N O L A E E
    E M W H I C H D R S N
S R T R Y M N S R A E S E
T E D G I F I R T T M O O
J E S U S M D E I O S R M
R Y A W I E T S D T R R F
N A R K K D M P N E U Y D
R N K S N E L A T O U E
    G A L V T Q A T L E
    U I M A L A M T
      T P H G E S
```

Answers

Picture Crossword

Star and Box

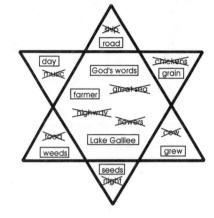

Find Two the Same

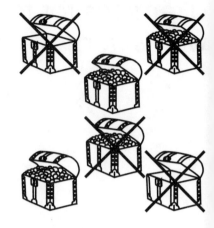

Marriage Maze

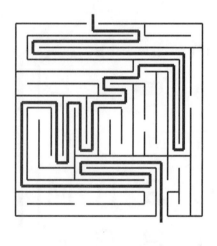

Dot-to-Dot

Stop and Search

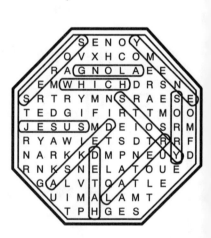

The Answer Is . . .:
The question is: Who comes to visit? The answer is: a friend.
The question is: What do you knock on? The answer is: the door.
The question is: What are you out of? The answer is: bread.
The question is: What do you have? The answer is: a problem.
The question is: What does your friend say? The answer is: Go away.

Dots and Lines: God is like the master. When you ask, God will forgive you.

Numbers and Letters: "It is foolish to love money more than you love God."

Silly Sacks: There are 18 sacks.